FastForward™

Riffs, Chords & Tricks 'n today!

Rock Guitar Improvisation

with Rikky Rooksby

Wise Publications

London / New York / Sydney / Paris / Copenhagen / Madrid

Exclusive Distributors:
Music Sales Limited
Distribution Centre, Newmarket Road, Bury St Edmunds,
Suffolk IP33 3YB, UK.
Music Sales Corporation
257 Park Avenue South, New York, NY10010, USA.
Music Sales Pty Limited
20 Resolution Drive, Caringbah, NSW 2229, Australia.

Order No. AM953250
ISBN 0-7119-7831-X
This book © Copyright 1999 by Wise Publications.

Written and arranged by Rikky Rooksby.
Music processed by Paul Ewers Music Design.
Cover photography courtesy of Balafon Books.

Text photographs courtesy of
London Features International & Redferns.

Printed and bound in the United Kingdom.

Your Guarantee of Quality:
As publishers, we strive to produce every book to
the highest commercial standards.
The music has been freshly engraved and the book has
been carefully designed to minimise awkward page turns
and to make playing from it a real pleasure.
Particular care has been given to specifying acid-free,
neutral-sized paper made from pulps which have not
been elemental chlorine bleached.
This pulp is from farmed sustainable forests and
was produced with special regard for the environment.
Throughout, the printing and binding have
been planned to ensure a sturdy, attractive publication
which should give years of enjoyment.
If your copy fails to meet our high standards, please
inform us and we will gladly replace it.

Guitar Tablature Explained

Guitar music can be notated three different ways: on a musical stave, in tablature, and in rhythm slashes

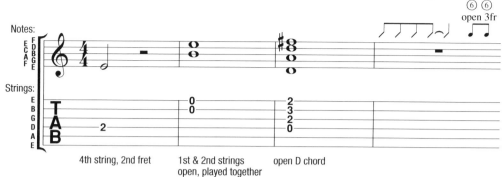

RHYTHM SLASHES are written above the stave. Strum chords in the rhythm indicated. Round noteheads indicate single notes.

THE MUSICAL STAVE shows pitches and rhythms and is divided by lines into bars. Pitches are named after the first seven letters of the alphabet.

TABLATURE graphically represents the guitar fingerboard. Each horizontal line represents a string, and each number represents a fret.

4th string, 2nd fret   1st & 2nd strings open, played together   open D chord

definitions for special guitar notation

SEMI-TONE BEND: Strike the note and bend up a semi-tone (1/2 step).

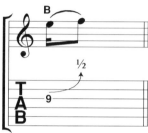

WHOLE-TONE BEND: Strike the note and bend up a whole-tone (whole step).

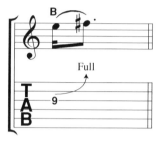

GRACE NOTE BEND: Strike the note and bend as indicated. Play the first note as quickly as possible.

QUARTER-TONE BEND: Strike the note and bend up a 1/4 step.

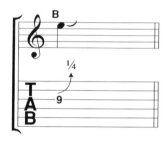

BEND & RELEASE: Strike the note and bend up as indicated, then release back to the original note.

COMPOUND BEND & RELEASE: Strike the note and bend up and down in the rhythm indicated.

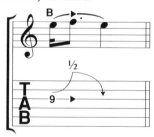

PRE-BEND: Bend the note as indicated, then strike it.

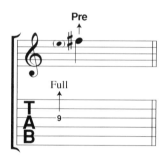

PRE-BEND & RELEASE: Bend the note as indicated. Strike it and release the note back to the original pitch.

UNISON BEND: Strike the two notes simultaneously and bend the lower note up to the pitch of the higher.

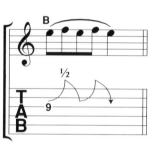

BEND & RESTRIKE: Strike the note and bend as indicated then restrike the string where the symbol occurs.

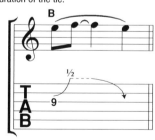

BEND, HOLD AND RELEASE: Same as bend and release but hold the bend for the duration of the tie.

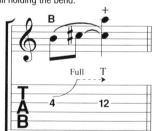

BEND AND TAP: Bend the note as indicated and tap the higher fret while still holding the bend.

VIBRATO: The string is vibrated by rapidly bending and releasing the note with the fretting hand.

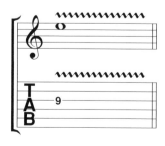

HAMMER-ON: Strike the first (lower) note with one finger, then sound the higher note (on the same string) with another finger by fretting it without picking.

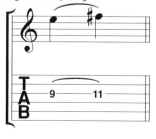

PULL-OFF: Place both fingers on the notes to be sounded, Strike the first note and without picking, pull the finger off to sound the second (lower) note.

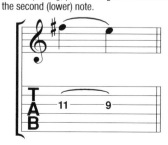

LEGATO SLIDE (GLISS): Strike the first note and then slide the same fret-hand finger up or down to the second note. The second note is not struck.

NOTE: The speed of any bend is indicated by the music notation and tempo.

SHIFT SLIDE (GLISS & RESTRIKE): Same as legato slide, except the second note is struck.

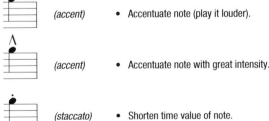

TRILL: Very rapidly alternate between the notes indicated by continuously hammering on and pulling off.

TAPPING: Hammer ("tap") the fret indicated with the pick-hand index or middle finger and pull off to the note fretted by the fret hand.

PICK SCRAPE: The edge of the pick is rubbed down (or up) the string, producing a scratchy sound.

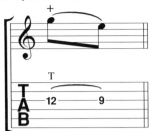

MUFFLED STRINGS: A percussive sound is produced by laying the fret hand across the string(s) without depressing, and striking them with the pick hand.

NATURAL HARMONIC: Strike the note while the fret-hand lightly touches the string directly over the fret indicated.

Harm.

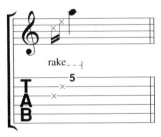

PINCH HARMONIC: The note is fretted normally and a harmonic is produced by adding the edge of the thumb or the tip of the index finger of the pick hand to the normal pick attack.

P.H.

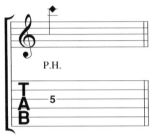

HARP HARMONIC: The note is fretted normally and a harmonic is produced by gently resting the pick hand's index finger directly above the indicated fret (in parentheses) while the pick hand's thumb or pick assists by plucking the appropriate string.

H.H.

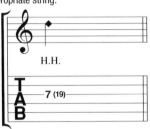

PALM MUTING: The note is partially muted by the pick hand lightly touching the string(s) just before the bridge.

P.M.

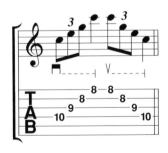

RAKE: Drag the pick across the strings indicated with a single motion.

rake

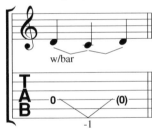

TREMOLO PICKING: The note is picked as rapidly and continuously as possible.

ARPEGGIATE: Play the notes of the chord indicated by quickly rolling them from bottom to top.

SWEEP PICKING: Rhythmic downstroke and/or upstroke motion across the strings.

VIBRATO DIVE BAR AND RETURN: The pitch of the note or chord is dropped a specific number of steps (in rhythm) then returned to the original pitch.

w/bar

VIBRATO BAR SCOOP: Depress the bar just before striking the note, then quickly release the bar.

w/bar

VIBRATO BAR DIP: Strike the note and then immediately drop a specific number of steps, then release back to the original pitch.

w/bar

additional musical definitions

(accent)	•	Accentuate note (play it louder).
(accent)	•	Accentuate note with great intensity.
(staccato)	•	Shorten time value of note.
⊓	•	Downstroke
V	•	Upstroke

D.%. al Coda

• Go back to the sign (%), then play until the bar marked ***To Coda*** ⊕ then skip to the section marked ⊕ ***Coda***.

D.C. al Fine

• Go back to the beginning of the song and play until the bar marked ***Fine*** (end).

tacet

• Instrument is silent (drops out).

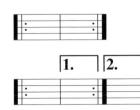

• Repeat bars between signs.

1. **2.**

• When a repeated section has different endings, play the first ending only the first time and the second ending only the second time.

Introduction

Hello, and welcome to ▶▶**Fast***Forward*.

Congratulations on purchasing a product that will improve your playing and provide you with hours of pleasure. All the music in this book has been specially created by professional musicians to give you maximum value and enjoyment.

If you already know how to 'drive' your instrument, but you'd like to do a little customising, you've pulled in at the right place. We'll put you on the fast track to playing the kinds of riffs and patterns that today's professionals rely on.

We'll provide you with a vocabulary of riffs and licks that you can apply in a wide variety of musical situations, with a special emphasis on giving you the techniques that will help you in a band situation.

▶▶**Fast***Forward* Rock Guitar Improvisation looks at everything from scales, bends, arpeggios and dynamics, to how to begin and end a solo, how to use intervals and phrasing, and gives you a host of other tips for effective rock lead. If you've been playing for about 6 months to a year, can change chords reasonably well, and have tried a few scales, this is the book that will take you further. If you are a beginner or new to lead playing, I recommend that you get a copy of Lead Guitar Licks in the ▶▶**Fast***Forward* series.

All the music examples in this book come with full-band audio tracks so that you get your chance to join in. Practise and learn the examples and then take off on your own over the backing tracks!

All players and bands get their sounds and styles by drawing on the same basic building blocks. With ▶▶**Fast***Forward* you'll quickly learn these, and then be ready to use them to create your own style.

Playing A Solo

Imagine you're in a recording studio. The red light is on, there's a session in progress. You can just about make out the faces of the engineer and the other band members behind the glass. You're holding a guitar, and through your headphones you're listening to the tracks for a newly-recorded song. Verses and choruses pass by, and soon… very soon… it will be time to record a solo. How confident would you feel about playing the session?

▶▶**Fast*Forward*** Rock Guitar Improvisation will help you to create fantastic lead guitar breaks and fills. No-one can teach you how to play an inspired solo - however, you can learn a lot about technique and musical sense to give you a better chance of playing one.

The book is divided into five sections. Each section represents a different recording session and a different rock number. Before each solo, you get to play a few simple phrases at a slow tempo, practise some scale-type patterns and try some other ideas that you could use in a solo of your own. Then it's your chance to learn a solo (usually 24 bars) that fits the chord sequence. Later, you can use the backing tracks to improvise your own lead breaks. Each solo is accompanied by a 'Spotlight on Technique', which focuses on the lead ideas featured in the solo.

Along the way this book will answer some of the common questions players have about lead guitar:

What scales should I be using?

Do I have to change the scale when the chord changes?

Which scales go with rock? Are these the same as for other styles of music?

When should I use string-bending?

Which scales go with which key?

How do I make the scales I know sound more like a solo?

Each example is given in musical score and in guitar tablature. With the latter each number indicates the fret at which the note is played, each line is a string. If you find it hard to remember which way up they go, think always of pitch: high notes are above low notes, therefore the highest sounding string (1st E) is at the top.

Each musical example is played once with the lead guitar, and once without. The first is for you to learn by listening, the second 'play-along' track is for you to practise with. The examples have a one-bar count-in on the CD.

TRACK I Tuning notes

▶▶ JIMI HENDRIX
"There's so many different things we do and nothing is never the same each night...'cos it's... improvised, you know, almost like a free feeling..."

nto The Great Wide Yonder
Pentatonic Scale Shapes

Playing good solos depends on musical understanding. It's not only what you know, but knowing how to apply it.

The most popular type of scale for lead soloing in rock and blues is the pentatonic scale: the name means 'five notes'. In the first session, we'll be using this scale in its minor form in the key of A.

To get you started, Exercise 1 has some simple phrases based on this scale, without any bends. Look out for the slide and pull-off in bar 7. Otherwise it's nice and easy.

TRACKS 2+3

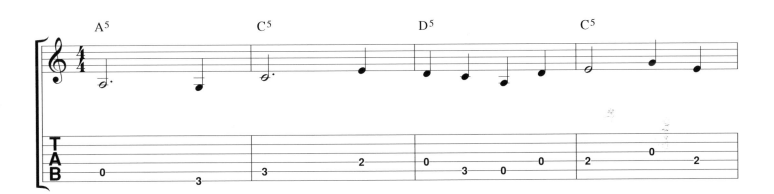

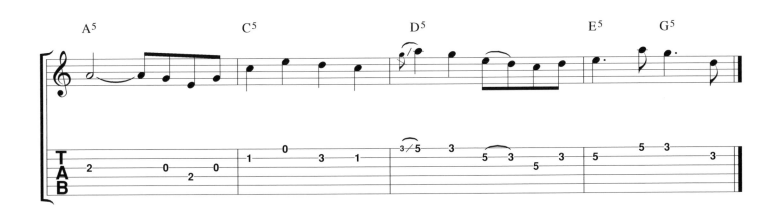

Pentatonic Scale Patterns

Exercise 2 takes you through a number of positions in which this scale can be played. You'll notice that bars 1, 3, 5 and 7 have the same notes but are played with a different fingering. When soloing, use whichever fingering works best with what you are playing - sometimes you'll need to play in different positions on the neck.

Unlike standard scale patterns, these patterns don't go all the way across the neck from the bottom string to the top. When you're playing lead you'll concentrate on higher pitched notes, to cut across the sound of the rest of the band.

Although this example is set around A, remember that these patterns can be shifted up or down to enable you to play in a different key. All you need to do is locate the note A in any given bar and use that as a 'marker note'. You can then simply move the pattern up or down until the marker note has become the note of the key you want to play in and the rest of the pattern will look after itself.

TRACKS 4+5

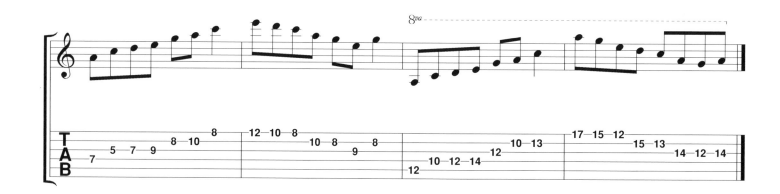

Slides And Bends

Now that you've practised a few patterns, it's time to look at what you can do with them. A lead guitar solo is much more than a scale or a fragment of a scale - they're just the bricks from which the solo is built. To make a solo work, you need to combine the notes in ways that are melodically and rhythmically interesting.

To decorate the basic notes of the scale, players use techniques like the slide, hammer-on, pull-off

and bend. In Exercise 3, you have a chance to apply slides and bends to some pentatonic minor patterns. Bars 1-2 feature 4 slides. Bars 3-4 feature the same note with bends substituted for slides. Notice the difference in the sound. Pay particular attention to the bends in bars 5-8 - these are extremely common and can be used in many different ways. Listen to your bends and try to ensure that you bend by the right amount so that the note at the top of the bend is in tune.

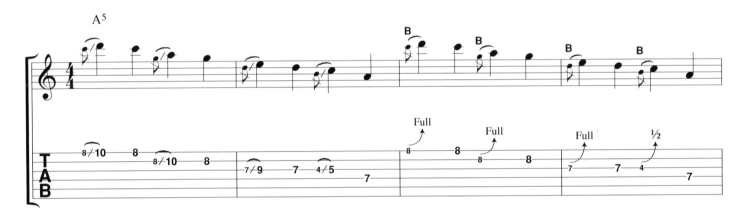

Now we come to the first solo, where you can try out some of the patterns and bends that you've been working on. 'Into The Great Wide Yonder' (Exercise 4) is a 24-bar solo with a four-bar riff intro/outro, which copies a real musical situation where you will be playing chords or a riff before you get to the solo itself.

The backing uses what rock musicians call 'power-chords'. These chords are properly known as 'fifths'.

Each consists of only two notes, whereas a full major or minor chord requires three. The note that tells you whether the chord would be major or minor is absent. This gives the music that distinctive 'tough' rock sound.

Here's our first ▶▶Spotlight On Techniques, where we look at particular ideas in the solo which you can learn and then use in your own:

▶▶Spotlight On Techniques

Slides:-
You will find the slides in bars 7 and 8 easiest to do with the third finger.

Pull-offs:-
With the pull-offs in bars 15 and 21-23, remember to keep the first finger secure at the lower fret where the pull-off will finish. Watch out for the less common pull-offs onto open strings in bar 11.

Hammer-on/Pull-off:-
The two techniques are combined in bar 28. This technique gives you more notes for fewer strokes of the picking hand.

Bends:-
Half-step bends occur in bar 13, while full bends occur in bars 15-20. Watch out for the bend in bar 24 which drops back via a half bend from a full bend.

Unison bend:-
This is a special type of bend in which you bend a note up whilst holding the same note on the string above. You end up with two notes at the same pitch. It produces a characteristic 'thickening' of the sound. There are unison bends

in bars 25-27. Experiment by moving these up or down the neck.

Double-stops:-
Solos don't have to be entirely made up of single notes. Sometimes it's good to play two notes at once, as in bar 14.

Harmony:-
The musical value of any note(s) you play depends on the chord that you're playing over. Sometimes you don't need to play different notes, you can repeat a note or a phrase over a chord-change. The change of chord will give the same phrase another 'colour'. Examples include bars 17-18 and 21-22.

Phrasing:-
Solos benefit from having certain phrases repeated. This gives the listener a chance to recognise something he or she has already heard. Bars 5-6 and 9-10 use this technique.

If you can play your way through 'Into The Great Wide Yonder', why not try taking some of these ideas and make up a solo of your own over the backing track?

▶▶ *SLASH (GUNS N' ROSES)*
"It's not so much how good a player you are, it's how cool you are."

Into The Great Wide Yonder

TRACKS 8+9

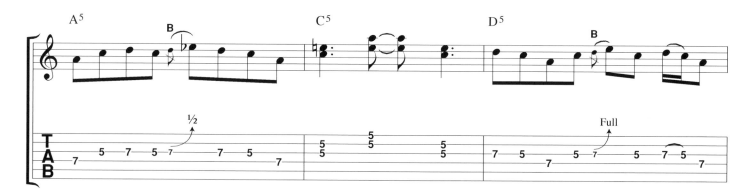

► ► **JAMES DEAN BRADFIELD (MANIC STREET PREACHERS)**
"I wanted to be someone like Napoleon. Then I discovered music - or The Clash to be more precise - and that was it. My destiny was determined."

Interstate Highway
Major Scale Phrases

For the next example we're moving into a major key.

Try Exercise 5, which is at the same slow tempo as Exercise 1, and listen to the difference in feel caused by changing from minor to major. There are no bends, just two slides, in bars 3 and 8.

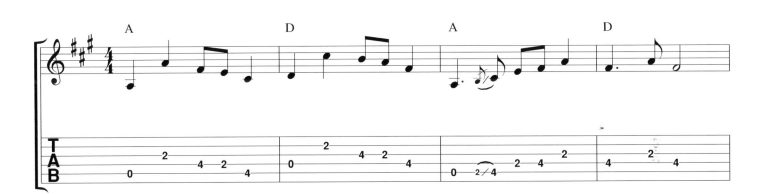

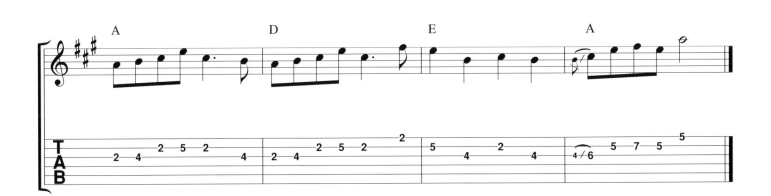

Major Scale Patterns

Exercise 6 demonstrates a variety of pentatonic major patterns, open string and fretted, similar to the pentatonic minor in Exercise 1. Being major, this scale has a happier, more upbeat mood. Try to make sure the changes between positions and the picking are as smooth as you can get them. Don't get behind the beat - but don't get ahead of it either!

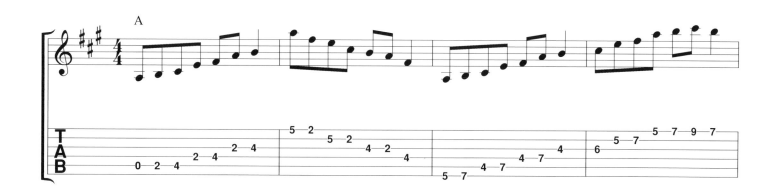

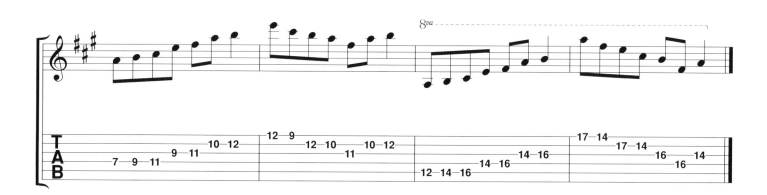

Major Pentatonic Patterns

Exercise 7 shows you some of the things you can do with these major pentatonic patterns, based on slides and bends. Some of the physical shapes involved are exactly the same as for the pentatonic minor but they sound completely different because in a different position on the fretboard they create different notes.

TRACKS 14+15

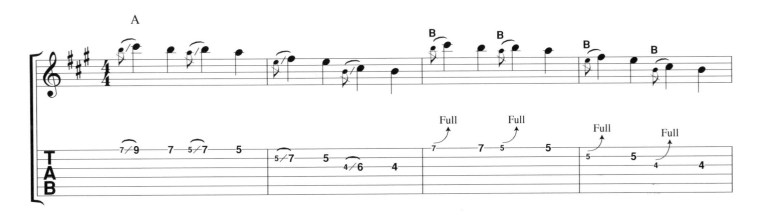

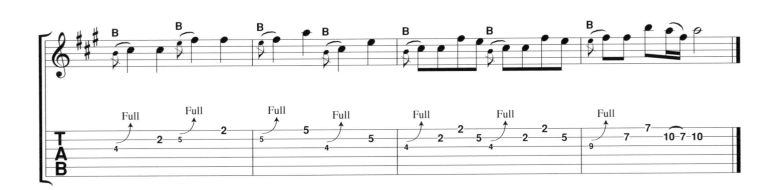

'Interstate Highway' (Exercise 8) is a 24-bar solo with a four-bar chordal intro. The backing uses a mixture of power-chords and major chords. The major chords give the music a more upbeat sound than 'Into The Great Wide Yonder'.

▶▶Spotlight On Techniques

Slides:-
The slides in bars 16 and 27 should be executed with the third finger. Those in bars 19, 20, and 28 require the second finger because that will set you up nicely in position for the notes that follow.

Pull-offs:-
Notice the difference in speed between the rapid pull-off in bar 13 and the slower one in bar 22. Bar 13 is easier if you barre the top two strings at the fifth fret.

Hammer-on/Pull-off:-
Notice the rapid hammer-ons in bars 5, 9 and 14, compared to the slower one in bar 10.

Bends:-
Half-step bends occur in bars 22 and 26; full bends in bars 11, 17, 19-21, 23, and 29. Be careful to get them in tune by bending by the right amount.

Chordal bend:-
The bend in bar 11 actually results in a D major triad if you allow all the notes in the bar to ring. Bend with your third finger and hold the top two notes with the little finger. Make sure the third finger is supported by putting your first and second fingers on the 7th and 8th frets of the third string. This means you can push with three fingers instead of one. The last bar has a bend which strongly suggests the chord of A major.

Double-stops:-
Notice how the double-stops in bar 18 and bar 23 (a classic rock'n'roll example) make the lead solo sound heavier.

Harmony:-
The double-stop in bar 18 clearly follows the chord change and therefore supports the harmony. This is very useful if you're playing in a rock trio without keyboards or rhythm guitar.

Repeat lick:-
A repeat lick is any short phrase which takes a few notes and then repeats them. The art of using a repeat lick is to know how many times you can do it without getting boring. The repeat lick is a special instance of the principle of repetition: give the audience something they can recognise. There's a repeat lick in bars 23-24.

Phrasing:-
Notice how bars 5-12 are built around a single pentatonic pattern. Remember, it's important to think about how to begin and end your solo. This solo starts with a single held note but the rapid hammer-on gives it extra emphasis.

▶▶ **KURT COBAIN (NIRVANA)**
"Punk rock should mean freedom...accepting everything that you like and playing everything that you like as sloppy as you like, as long as it's good and has passion."

Interstate Highway

▶▶ **PAUL WELLER**
"Hopefully being moved by music is a process that will always happen - the day you don't get inspired by something is when you know it's all over."

▶▶ FastForward™
Guide To Guitar

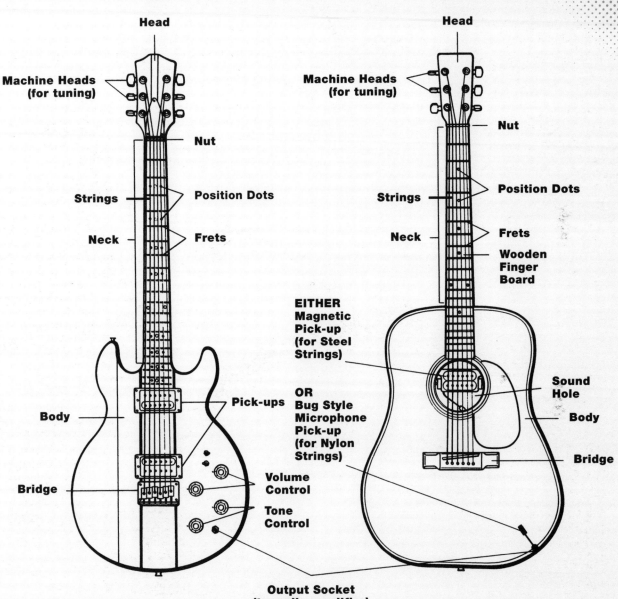

Head

Machine Heads (for tuning)

Nut

Strings

Position Dots

Neck

Frets

EITHER Magnetic Pick-up (for Steel Strings)

OR Bug Style Microphone Pick-up (for Nylon Strings)

Pick-ups

Body

Volume Control

Bridge

Tone Control

Output Socket (to audio amplifier)

Head

Machine Heads (for tuning)

Nut

Strings

Position Dots

Neck

Frets

Wooden Finger Board

Sound Hole

Body

Bridge

The Guitar

Whether you have an acoustic or an electric guitar, the principles of playing are fundamentally the same, and so are most of the features on both instruments.

In order to 'electrify' an acoustic guitar (as in the diagram), a magnetic pick up can be attached to those guitars with steel strings or a 'bug' style microphone pick-up can be attached to guitars with nylon strings.

If in doubt check with your local music shop.

Tuning Your Guitar

Tuning
Accurate tuning of the guitar is essential, and is achieved by winding the machine heads up or down. It is always better to 'tune up' to the correct pitch rather than down.

Therefore, if you find that the pitch of your string is higher (sharper) than the correct pitch, you should 'wind down' below the correct pitch, and then 'tune up' to it.

Relative Tuning
Tuning the guitar to itself without the aid of a pitch pipe or other tuning device.

Other Methods Of Tuning
Pitch pipe
Tuning fork
Dedicated electronic guitar tuner

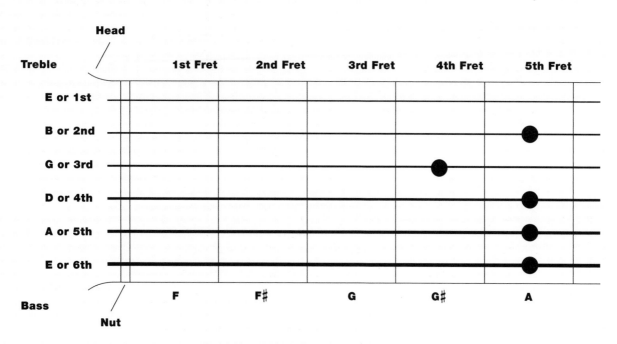

● Press down where indicated, one at a time, following the instructions below.

Estimate the pitch of the 6th string as near as possible to **E** or at least a comfortable pitch (not too high or you might break other strings in tuning up).

Then, while checking the various positions on the above diagram, place a finger from your left hand on:

- The 5th fret of the E or 6th string and **tune the open A** (or 5th string) to the note (A)

- The 5th fret of the A or 5th string and **tune the open D** (or 4th string) to the note (D)

- The 5th fret of the D or 4th string and **tune the open G** (or 3rd string) to the note (G)

- The 4th fret of the G or 3rd string and **tune the open B** (or 2nd string) to the note (B)

- The 5th fret of the B or 2nd string and **tune the open E** (or 1st string) to the note (E)

Chord Boxes

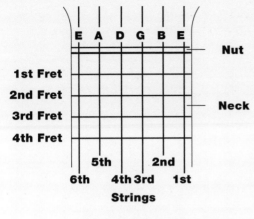

E A D G B E

Nut

1st Fret

2nd Fret

Neck

3rd Fret

4th Fret

5th   2nd

6th   4th 3rd   1st

Strings

The A Chord

6 5 4 3 2 1   Frets

1st

① ② ③   2nd

3rd

4th

5th

x

x = do not play this string

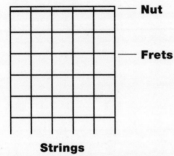

Nut

Frets

Strings

Chord boxes are diagrams of the guitar neck viewed head upwards, face on, as illustrated in the above drawings. The horizontal double line at the top is the nut, the other horizontal lines are the frets. The vertical lines are the strings starting from E or 6th on the left to E or 1st on the right.

Any dots with numbers inside them simply indicate which finger goes where. Any strings marked with an **x** must not be played.

The fingers of your hand are numbered 1, 2, 3, & 4 as in the diagram below.

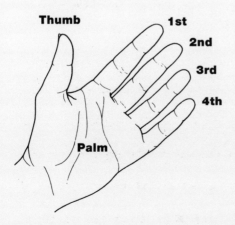

Thumb   1st

2nd

3rd

4th

Palm

All chords are major chords unless otherwise indicated.

Left Hand
Place all three fingers into position and press down firmly. Keep your thumb around the middle of the back of the neck and directly behind your 1st and 2nd fingers.

Right Hand Thumb Or Plectrum
Slowly play each string, starting with the 5th or A string and moving up to the 1st or E string.

If there is any buzzing, perhaps you need to:-
Position your fingers nearer the metal fret (towards you); or adjust the angle of your hand; or check that the buzz is not elsewhere on the guitar by playing the open strings in the same manner.

Finally, your nails may be too long, in which case you are pressing down at an extreme angle and therefore not firmly enough. Also the pad of one of your fingers may be in the way of the next string for the same reason.

So, cut your nails to a more comfortable length and then try to keep them as near vertical to the fretboard as possible.

Once you have a 'buzz-free' sound, play the chord a few times and then remove your fingers and repeat the exercise until your positioning is right instinctively.

Holding The Guitar

The picture above shows a comfortable position for playing rock or pop guitar

The Right Hand
When STRUMMING (brushing your fingers across the strings), hold your fingers together.

When PICKING (plucking strings individually), hold your wrist further away from the strings than for strumming.

Keep your thumb slightly to the left of your fingers which should be above the three treble strings as shown.

The Plectrum
Many modern guitar players prefer to use a plectrum to strike the strings. Plectrums come in many sizes, shapes and thicknesses and are available from your local music shop.

Start with a fairly large, soft one if possible, with a grip. The photo shows the correct way to hold your plectrum.

The Left Hand
Use your fingertips to press down on the strings in the positions described. Your thumb should be behind your 1st and 2nd fingers pressing on the middle of the back of the neck.

RM92051G

The Outsider
Major Scale Shapes

Now we'll explore some other possibilities in A
major. Exercise 9 is a melody using all the notes
of the major scale. As before, listen to the tonal
difference of what you're playing.

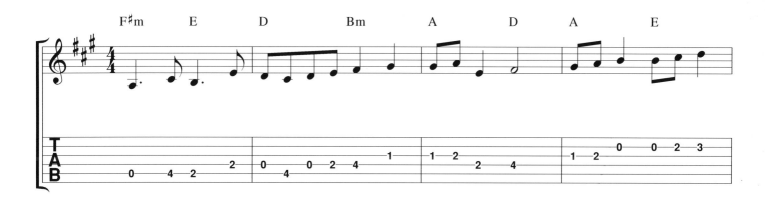

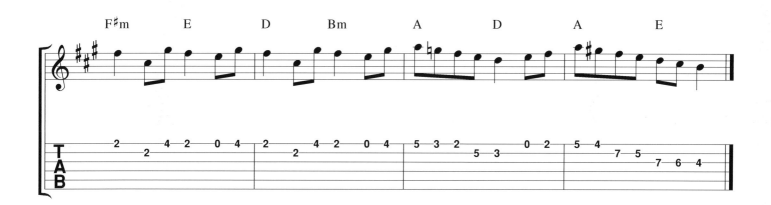

The Mixolydian Mode

Exercise 10 begins with the scale of A major with the root note on the open 5th string. A major has 7 notes in contrast to the pentatonic's five. Let's compare them:

A pentatonic major = A B C♯   E F♯
A major =   A B C♯ D E F♯ G♯

The pentatonic major is simply an 'edited' version of the major scale, and like its pentatonic sibling, the full major scale has a happier mood.

In the even-numbered bars you'll notice that the G♯ of the major scale is flattened to G natural. This turns the major scale into another, known as

the mixolydian mode. This alteration is very common in rock music. When you remember that it is only this note which is different you will find it easier to use both scales.

To turn the A major scale pattern into A mixolydian, or vice versa, simply locate any Gs and play them either sharp or natural depending on which scale you want. If you glance back at Exercise 9 you'll notice you played a G natural in bar 7 and a G♯ in bar 8 for contrast.

TRACKS 20+21

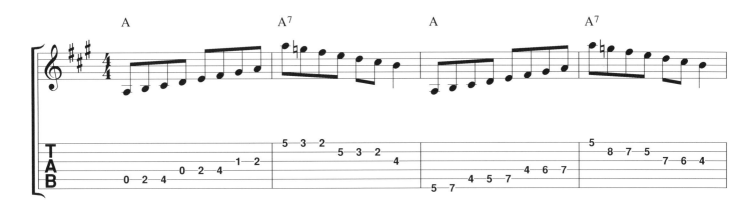

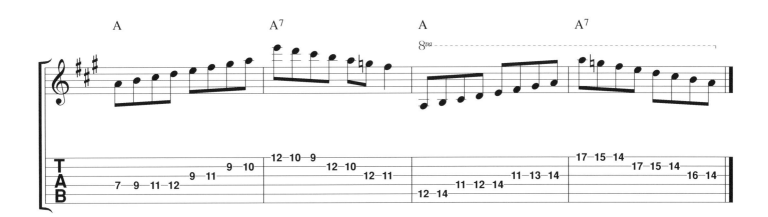

Using Open Strings

So far we've been thinking about scales and single-note patterns, but of course in a solo you can play more than one note at a time. Exercise 11 shows you how to move up and down a fretted string whilst hitting an open string above or below it. The basic rule is that the open string needs to have some relationship with the chord over which you're playing. In the first two bars the open string E is part of the A chord, the open string B in bars 3-4 is the root note of B

minor, the open string D in bars 5-6 is the root of D major, and finally the open string B in bars 7-8 is part of the chord of E major. In all cases the fretted notes are taken from the scale of A major, whichever string you're moving up and down.

The great thing about using open strings in this way is that it makes a much fuller sound, another useful trick for the guitarist in a rock trio.

TRACKS 22+23

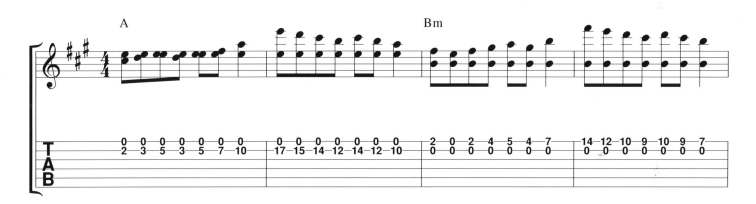

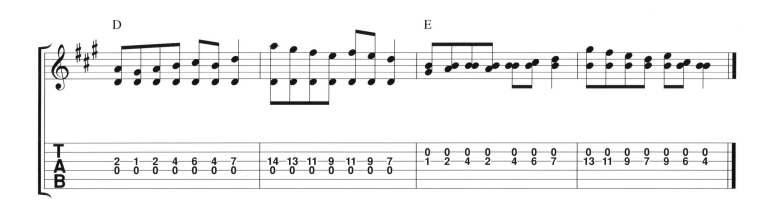

'The Outsider' (Exercise 12) is a 24-bar solo with a four-bar arpeggio intro played twice. The backing uses a mixture of major and minor chords. The presence of the minor chords in particular makes it difficult to use the A pentatonic major. (Try playing that scale over the backing track and you'll see what I mean, it sounds flat.)

▶▶Spotlight On Techniques

Bends:-

Be careful not to over-bend the half-step bends in bars 6, 10, 11 and 27. Remember to support the third finger for the full bends in bar 12, 22-27.

Chordal bend:-

As with the previous solo, there's a chordal bend to finish, emphasising the A major chord.

Open strings:-

This solo makes a special feature of using fretted notes and an open string. The open B string supports the fretted notes above it against the Bm chord in bars 13-14 and 17-18, with the open string E doing the same job against the F♯m and C♯m chords in bars 15-16 and 19-20.

Harmonics:-

To produce these 'ghostly' notes hold a finger against the string right over the fretwire of whichever fret you need, being careful not to press the string against the fingerboard. Once you've struck the string, pull your finger away to let the string resonate. Inserted unexpectedly into a solo, harmonics can be quite a surprise! See bars 11 and 21.

Phrasing:-

Compare bar 5 with 21. It's the same melodic idea one octave higher. Re-stating a melodic idea is a good way of giving a solo structure.

▶▶ **THE EDGE (U2)**
"I don't think that U2 will ever get to the stage where there's a formula, our way of writing is always so much a part of experimenting, and a feeling at the time... there are no rules to what we do."

The Outsider

TRACKS 24+25

▶▶ *NOEL GALLAGHER (OASIS)*
"I'm a songwriter. I'm more of a strummer than a lead guitarist."
... but when Noel does take a solo, he favours the major pentatonic scale.

Summer Girl

Minor Key Phrases

Having looked at pentatonic patterns, the major
scale and the mixolydian mode, it's time to move
into the melancholy tone of the minor key.
Exercise 13 has a striking contrast of effect
depending on whether you play F or F♯.

TRACKS 26+27

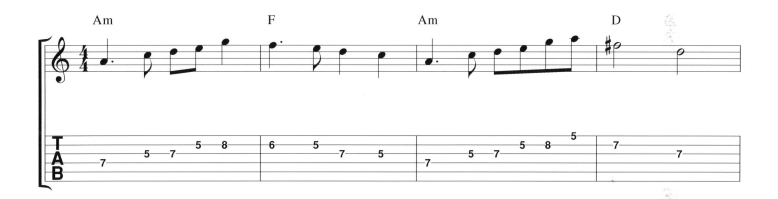

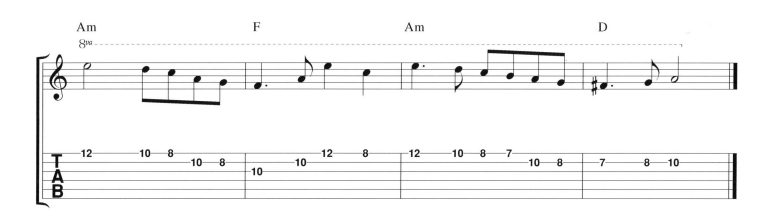

The Natural Minor Scale

Exercise 14 shows you some patterns that fit a minor key. In this exercise you first play the scale of A natural minor, also known as the aeolian mode. Modes are simply scales which date back to the classical world. Our major and minor scales are modes, and there are other modes which are not as well-known as these (but still used in Western music). Let's compare scales again:

A pentatonic minor = A   C D E   G

A natural minor
(aeolian mode) =   A B C D E F G

The pentatonic minor can be thought of as an edited natural minor scale.

If the sixth note (F) is sharpened (F♯) you create what is known as the A dorian mode. Each bar in Exercise 10 alternates between the melancholy aeolian mode and the slightly more angular dorian. Which scale you use over a given backing will depend on the chord sequence. Of course, you can use A pentatonic minor as well.

If you check Exercise 13 again, you'll now understand why you were playing F in some bars and F♯ in others. It all depends on the chord you're playing over. A chord of D (bars 4 and 8 of Exercise 13) needs F♯ rather than F, but F♯ would sound terrible over the F chord (bars 2 and 6).

TRACKS 28+29

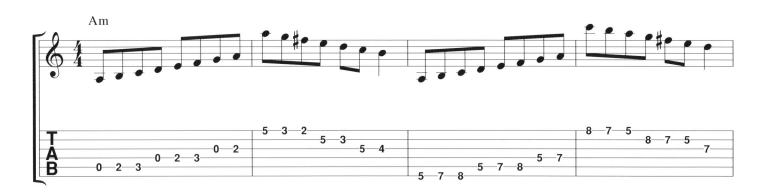

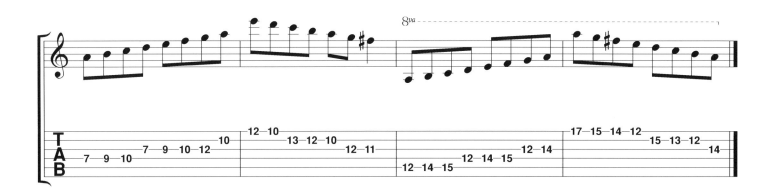

Hammer-Ons And Pull-Offs

Exercise 15 gives you the opportunity to practise two techniques. Bars 1-4 are a sequence of intervals known as '3rds'. Each pair of notes is quite close together, either two tones (major 3rd) or 1½ tones (minor 3rd). They have quite a sweet and full sound, and can be placed in a solo, as long as you use 3rds that belong to the scale (major or minor) of the key in which you're playing.

Bars 5-8 feature an extended hammer-on/pull-off figure - strike the first note and then produce the next three or four simply by using the fingers of the fretting hand.

TRACKS 30+31

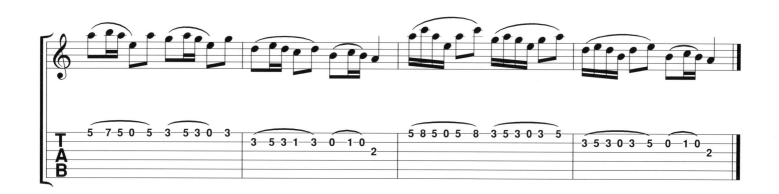

► *JIMMY PAGE (LED ZEPPELIN)*
"It's just a chord or riff that inspires me and then I go on and see how it goes colour-wise. The whole thing just grows like an acorn or something. I'm not a natural musician, I really have to practise damned hard to get anything out."

'Summer Girl' (Exercise 16) is a 24-bar solo in A minor with a four-bar chordal intro. The backing uses a mixture of minor and major chords, but because the music is in a minor key the music sounds emotionally sad. Most of the techniques are things you've already tried, so aim for a really convincing performance, and then try improvising a solo of your own over the backing track.

▶▶Spotlight On Techniques

Harmony:-

This solo is a good example of a musical situation in which you need both the aeolian and the dorian modes to fit the chord sequence. The dorian is easy to spot because you'll see F# in the music instead of plain F. Bars 5-12 and 21 to the end feature a D major chord, so don't play the aeolian here as the F and F# will clash. Likewise, bars 13-20 feature an F chord, therefore the right scale is the aeolian (except for bar 19 where D7 occurs) because a dorian F# would clash with the Fmaj7 chord in the backing. Listen out for the distinctive emotional change in the music as it switches between the two modes.

Phrasing:-

Notice the dramatic effect of the rhythm in bar 17. Here a powerful accented rhythm in the lead guitar is itself backed up by the rhythm section. Bars 13 and 15 both make significant use of a rest on the beat, so that the lead phrase starts on an offbeat. You might also like to consider the variation between bars that are busy - where there are quite a few notes - and bars where there may only be a couple. This type of variety is also important.

Summer Girl

▶▶ *PETE TOWNSHEND*
"I figured that one day someone would fall in love with me because I was a genius guitar player... so when the other kids were out dancing or listening to records, I was learning the guitar."

Trucker's Delight
Alternating Key Phrases

Now let's move back into major tonality and combine everything that we've learned.

Exercise 17 demonstrates some simple phrases to let you hear the difference between pentatonic majors and minors of the same key-note. The sudden appearance of natural signs in bars 3-4 and 6 tells you straightaway that the tone has changed.

TRACKS 34+35

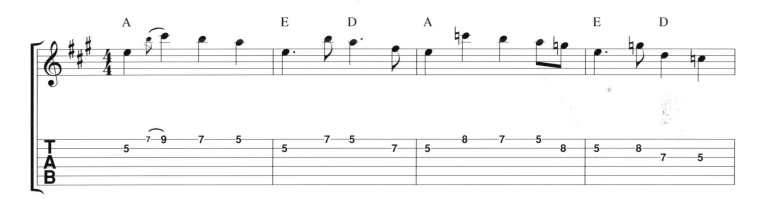

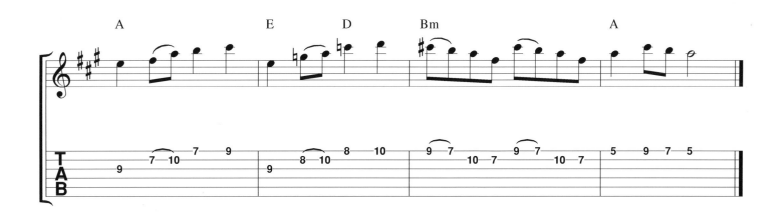

Pentatonic Major And Minor Patterns

Exercise 18 is designed to show you the way that the pentatonic minor and pentatonic major scale patterns actually overlap one another on the fretboard. This means that you can in fact switch scale without changing position.

TRACKS 36+37

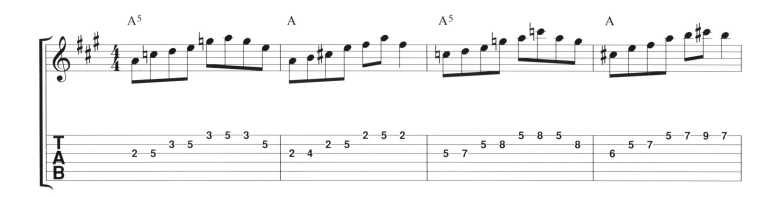

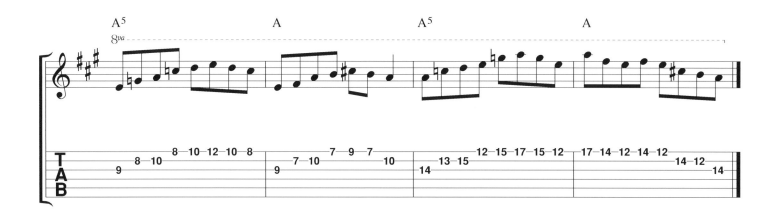

Arpeggio Shapes

Exercise 19 shows you some of the things you can do with arpeggios (rather than scale-based ideas). It uses some common triad chords on the top three strings which players often insert into solos. These reinforce the harmonic progression, and make a nice contrast with single note passages. Watch out for the 'rake' in bar 6 - to do this you push the pick up the strings so that the notes sound a split-second apart from each other. Alternatively, use the pick to strike the lowest note, and then your second and third fingers to pluck the next two, in a kind of rolling action.

TRACKS 38+39

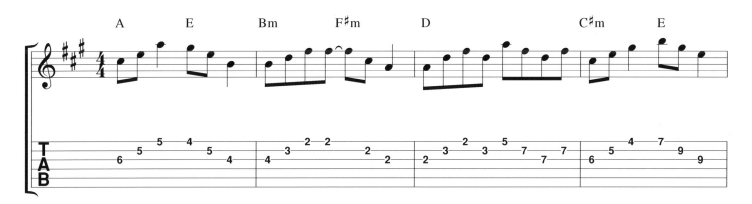

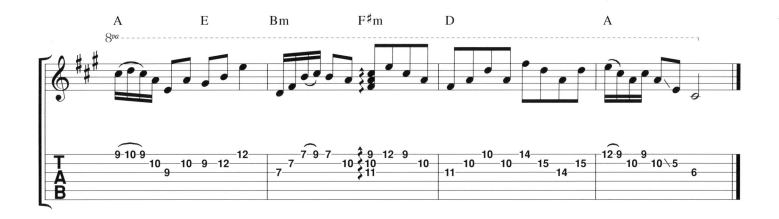

'Trucker's Delight' (Exercise 20) is a 33-bar solo. We're back in the key of A major, but with a twist - for at various points chords occur which are not strictly in the key. This means that the scales you would normally use may not fit; they can produce conspicuously wrong-sounding notes. These chords include the C♯ in bar 30, the C♯-F♯ in bars 6-7 and 14-15, and the chords in bars 17-20. This solo will show you how to cope with this kind of musical challenge.

▶▶Spotlight On Techniques

Slides:-

The slide in bar 26, with the third finger, helps to speed up the run.

Pull-offs:-

Watch out for the less common pull-off onto the open E string in bar 24.

Hammer-on:-

The hammer-ons in 29 and 30 help with the speed of the runs. Notice how the hammer-ons in 7 and 8 have a very bluesy sound, as you go from the natural note to the sharpened note.

Bends:-

Watch out for the unusual half-step bend in bar 2.

Unison bend:-

See bars 13-14 for a staggered unison bend, where the notes are hit one after the other.

Double-stops:-

The Chuck Berry-style double-stops occur in bars 9-12, and 15-16. Once you've lined up your first finger at the right fret, these are easy to move around as the chord changes. In bars 25 and 27 you'll find another two-note figure, this time with notes a sixth apart.

Harmony:-

The rapid chord change from F♯m to G in bar 31 is dealt with by using arpeggio figures. Bars 28 and 29 both kick-off with chordal/arpeggio ideas. Lead guitar doesn't have to be all scales!

Phrasing:-

In bar 19 you'll hear the phrase that was played in bar 17 re-fingered a few frets lower to fit the new chord. This is a handy technique for dealing with frequent awkward chord changes. The rest on the first beat of bars 25 and 27 gives a sense of surprise.

▶▶ **CRISPIAN MILLS (KULA SHAKER)**
"The whole thing about music isn't necessarily about how good you are, it's about what's driving you to be a musician."

Trucker's Delight

TRACKS 40+41

Conclusion

In these five Improvisation sessions you've covered a lot of ground. You've played solos in a variety of scales, including major and minor pentatonics, mixolydian, aeolian and dorian modes. You've experimented with open strings, hammer-ons, pull-offs and unison bends. You've also tried a few arpeggio figures and double-stops. When you're familiar with these techniques, listen to the solos again to get a sense of how one phrase develops and leads to another.

You will also have made another significant discovery. A solo may be made up of a series of little phrases and ideas, each of which may be easy to play on its own. However, playing them all one after the other, in time, without making a mistake, is another matter! If it seems hard at first, just keep at it, trying a few bars at a time. It will come - a little regular practice will bring rewards.

Now start trying your own ideas over the backing tracks, keeping in mind everything you've learnt. Have a look at some of the other great guitar books on our list to progress even further!

Essential Scales and Modes
CLM02503471
Forty-two moveable scales and modes arranged over rock, shuffle and funk grooves, including CD and performance notes.

Killer Pentatonics for Guitar
HLE00000148
Innovative and diverse ways of playing pentatonic scales in blues, rock and heavy metal.

Scales over Chords
BS70297
How to improvise lead lines over chord progressions and never play bad notes! A great way to supplement what you've learned in this book.

The Complete Rock Guitar Player
An exciting tutorial series based on classic rock and roll songs from top artists such as Eric Clapton, Jimi Hendrix, The Kinks, and David Bowie.

The Complete Rock Guitar Player Book 1
AM63934
The Complete Rock Guitar Player Book2
AM63942
The Complete Rock Guitar Player Book3
AM63959

First Guitar
With this excellent series you'll be playing great riffs and solos in no time. Clear instructions and diagrams in standard notation and guitar TAB.

First Guitar Lead Licks
AM953216
First Guitar Riffs
AM954184